sarahdateechur's guide to podcasting

A LITTLE SOMETHING FOR EDUCATORS WHO WANT TO GET STARTED (OR LEVEL UP)

(SERIES: SARAHDATEECHUR'S GUIDE TO...)
BOOK 1

SARAH THOMAS, PHD

Copyright © 2023 by Sarah Thomas
Published by EduMatch®
PO Box 150324, Alexandria, VA 22315
www.edumatchpublishing.com

All rights reserved. No portion of this book may be reproduced in any form without permission from the publisher, except as permitted by U.S. copyright law. For permissions contact sarah@edumatch.org.

These books are available at special discounts when purchased in quantities of 10 or more for use as premiums, promotions fundraising, and educational use. For inquiries and details, contact the publisher: sarah@edumatch.org.

ISBN: 978-1-959347-21-7

For Mom, Dad, Mike, and Grandma, who taught me how to use my voice.
For Keith and Kara, who give me a reason to sing.
For my PLF, with whom I learn and grow.
Thank you all and much love.

contents

1. Introduction — 1
2. Gearing Up — 11
3. Planning and Preparation — 27
4. Creation and Workflow — 35
5. Marketing and Promotion — 49
6. The Finish Line — 63

References — 71
Acknowledgments — 73
About the Author — 75
Also by Sarah Thomas, PhD — 77
Related EduMatch Titles — 83

ONE

introduction

H ello, everyone. Thank you so much for picking up a copy of *Sarahdateechur's Guide to Podcasting*. I'm super excited to have you join our family. My name is Sarah, and I'm going to be your *guide on the side*, your *hostess with the mostest*.

But guess what? This is all about YOU. This is all about your journey—but you're not alone. You have community members to your left and to your right, other people who are learning with you whom you will meet in our online community. We are a team. We're about to cross this finish line together.

Here is a quick heads-up on what to expect as you read this book. By the end, you're going to have your very first episode that you're going to put out there to the world. I'm super excited to hear what you have to share.

Module 1 will provide you with a basic introduction to this book, including some reasons why to podcast, and what to expect from the course as a whole.

Module 2 is all about gear. Whether you are a newbie or a seasoned professional, there's something for everyone ranging from how to start with what you already have to recommended upgrades.

Module 3 discusses planning and preparation for your podcast. As my dad used to tell me when I was a kid, "plan your work and work your plan." This section will tell you exactly how to do this, including finding guests and topics.

Module 4 talks about creation and workflow. How do you record? How do you edit? How do you troubleshoot situations where you and your guests may be in opposite time zones? Find out here.

Module 5 addresses what many find the most challenging part of podcasting: marketing and promotion. It's difficult to toot your own horn sometimes. Find out ways to do this painlessly and efficiently.

Finally, **Module 6** provides you with some food for thought, namely how to get the most bang for your buck. Here, we cover captions, repurposing content, and other ideas.

I have to admit, I'm doing this kind of selfishly because I am an avid listener of podcasts as well as an avid creator, and I want to hear more from my community members. So I wrote this book because I want to hear what you have to say. You want to share what you have to say, so this is a win-win.

WHY PODCAST?

At the time of this writing, I've been an educator for 18 years. I also run an organization called EduMatch, which facilitates grassroots connections among educators around the world. One of the branches of EduMatch is a publishing company, where we have published nearly 100 books (and counting).

Many times, prospective authors approach me and say that they have a story that they would like to write, but they think nobody will want to read it because there are other books on the same topic. My advice to them is always, *"Other people may have shared, but nobody will tell the story quite like you will."* We all have unique perspectives shaped by our backgrounds, life experiences, and other factors. Perhaps the way that you share your knowledge will resonate with someone in a way that is unmatched by anything else they have encountered.

The same can be said about podcasting.

Podcasting, in essence, is sharing through audio (and/or video). It's just another way to share a story, not much different than blogging. As a matter of fact, podcasting can complement blogging and book-writing very well, as we will see in Module Six. But what about on the consumer side?

Allow me to get a little bit geeky with some statistics. According to Ruby (2022), there are more than two million podcasts globally, with nearly 400 million listeners. Over 28% of the U.S. population listens to podcasts weekly, on average listening to eight shows. Wow, that's a lot. (Now I have to tell you, it's probably about eight a day for me.)

Those are some pretty heavy stats to digest. But that's good to know because this is a great way to get your message through to many people. Not only that, podcasting is super-accessible. I must tell you, my main time to listen to podcasts is usually when I'm on a run, doing dishes, driving in my car, or getting ready for work. Think about it for a second; when do you usually listen to podcasts?

The cool thing about educational podcasts is that you can get a lot of professional learning during times when you wouldn't necessarily do that. That's part of their appeal and what makes them so popular.

One more thing to keep in mind is that you may want to establish the mission and vision of your podcast. This may sound very corporate, but it is important for several reasons:

- Clarity: A clear mission and vision will give you clarity on what your podcast is all about, what you want to achieve, and who you want to serve.
- Direction: With a solid mission and vision, you'll always know in which direction you're headed and what decisions to make to stay true to your podcast's purpose.
- Consistency: When you know your mission and vision, it will be easier to make sure your episodes are consistent with your overall goal, and that each episode moves you closer to your vision.
- Purpose: Your mission and vision give your podcast purpose, making it more meaningful for you, and for your listeners.
- Differentiation: When you know your mission and vision, it will be easier to differentiate yourself from other podcasts, and to stand out in a crowded market.

Take some time to set out some goals, such as what you want to achieve and who you want to serve, and you will be on the right path to podcast success!

WHAT TO EXPECT

You may have just read that last section and said, "Hey, Sarah, that's great, but how do I do this thing?" Well, fear not, friends. That is why we have this book. That's exactly why we're here.

We're going to talk about how to podcast. We're going to talk about things going from hardware and software, to how to get guests and topics. In addition, we're going to discuss recording and editing—how to give it that little bit of polish you might want. We're also going to cover sharing and repurposing the content so you can have it in various formats.

Full transparency—I created a course by the same title, and most of this book was taken from the transcript. (Don't worry, I will teach you this trick later in the book.) If you want to access the course and see some of these principles in action, you can access the course entitled "Podcasting with your PLN" at edumatch.thinkific.com and take 50%

off with code COMMUNITYPODCASTING. However, even if you choose not to, I encourage you to access our community to share your learning and takeaways with our community. The direct link to do so is bit.ly/communitypodcasting.

Hopefully, by the time you finish this book, then…get ready for it…we'll launch episode one. Some of you may already have podcasts that are up and running and might be here to get some ideas about new things you want to try. I'm here for that as well! Welcome, and please share your experiences with the community so we can learn from you.

HOMEWORK: MEET YOUR TEAMMATES

One cool thing about this book is that, as I said before, you are not alone. We're in this together. You have people reading this book alongside you and some accessing the course (more on that later). So we're going in as a team—we're not leaving anybody behind. We're going to cross this finish line together. For this purpose, we have a community where you are invited to engage and interact.

Are you ready for your first piece of homework? I will challenge you to stop by and introduce yourself so we can get to know one another. So are you game? Are you down for the challenge? Let's go!

If you have not already done so, please head over to our community at bit.ly/communitypodcasting and introduce yourself to the community of learners there. Also, please set a goal you would like to achieve by the end of this book.

TWO

gearing up

This module will discuss the hardware and software involved in getting a good-quality podcast. We're also going to talk about different platforms.

Materials Needed

- Computer
- Microphone
- Headphones
- Webcam (optional)
- Podcasting Platform

M.V.P. AND MINDSET

Although hardware and software are important when creating your podcast, the result does not have to be perfect—it doesn't have to be polished. In the business world, there's something called MVP, which stands for a minimum viable product. The purpose of the MVP is to get something out there that we can refine, and that we improve based on feedback. As the old saying goes, perfect is the enemy of done.

As educators, we are familiar with grading scales. In the school district where I currently work, 90% is an A. 100%

is also an A, but that's a whole 10% difference. Tim Ferriss (2020) discussed the Pareto principle (also known as the 80-20 rule) for learning languages, with a goal of 95% fluency in three months. However, if he aimed for 98% fluency, this would likely take him ten years.

Keep this in mind when you are creating your podcast. You will have many years to refine it, but the important thing is to begin. Continuous improvement in podcasting is all about constantly spicing up the listener experience and raising the bar on your show's quality. As a podcaster, it's key to keep evolving and catering to your audience's needs. That's why it's crucial to involve your listeners in the process and get feedback from them. This module will help you get a jump start with a solid foundation.

Hopefully, you're going to have a lengthy podcasting career. After a few years, you can always go back and look at the very first and last episodes, and you'll be able to tell your growth over that whole trajectory.

The point of all this is to say that you don't have to worry about getting it perfect before you get it out there. Such is life—the journey of life is about constantly leveling up. As James Clear, the author of *Atomic Habits*, states, "If you master continuous improvement and get 1% better each day for one year, you'll end up 37 times better by the time you're done" (Clear, 2022).

"MY MIC SOUNDS NICE, CHECK ONE..."

That said, you don't have to break the bank when you think about your gear. You might already have everything you need to begin.

However, if you need to buy a microphone, you may want to think about a few things. One major thing is directionality, which basically means how the microphone picks up sounds. Different types are omnidirectional (picks up sound from all directions, which would be good to put in the middle of a group), unidirectional (picks up sound from one direction, which is ideal for solo podcasts), or bidirectional (picks up sound from two opposite directions, which works well in situations when you and your guest are facing one another).

You also want to decide, dynamic or condenser mic? Dynamic microphones are well-known for their strength and ability to handle high levels of sound pressure; plus, they're less susceptible to background noise, making them a great option for recording in less-than-perfect environments. Condenser microphones, on the other hand, are famous for their clarity and precision. They are more delicate to background noise, so they might not be the best pick for noisy recording locations.

Another thing to consider is connectivity. Are you recording straight to a computer? If so, chances are you may want to go with a USB microphone. If you're using another interface, such as a sound board, check to see if you need an XLR or phone plug connector.

Earbuds with built-in microphones tend to work well for basic voice recording and video conferencing. However, a dedicated microphone typically offers better sound quality and versatility.

The best microphone for you will depend on your specific needs, such as the type of recording, the environment, and your budget. If you are looking for a good quality microphone, I have heard some really good things about the Audio-Technica AT2005 microphone. It's what is known as a cardioid microphone, which is pretty good at picking up sound to the front and the sides. At the time of this writing, this microphone was priced just under $60. This may be a little pricey for just starting out, but you want to make sure to keep your audio clean, whatever it is that you do, meaning high-quality and free from unwanted noise like hisses, hums, crackles, and background noise. You want to make sure that it's not distorted or muffled, and that the levels don't go too high or too low.

As I said before, I listen to a lot of podcasts. The audio quality is of utmost importance. There have been some shows where I loved the hosts, but the audio wasn't clear. This frustrated me as a listener, so eventually, I just stopped listening. There have been some episodes of my own show where I've gone back and been like, "What is that noise?"

The microphone I currently use is a Blue Yeti X. At the time of writing, this is one of their newer models. So I have that one I take with me on the road. I also have two Blue Yeti Blackouts. (One of them I keep at my house, and the other one has a permanent home at my parents' house because they have better Wi-Fi—also very important!) These are high-quality microphones, but I did not start with them. Your microphone does not have to break the bank.

Quite honestly, you can often get clean audio from standard headphones with a microphone jack. I suggest that you first try with what you have. Don't go out spending hundreds and thousands of dollars to get the best possible mic. You might have something that most people won't be able to tell the difference for a lot cheaper. Then again, you might be a person who likes to splurge and drop money. If that's the case, don't let me tell you what to do, big baller! But for everyone else, don't feel like you have to go all out when you're first starting. I recommend using what you have first until you outgrow it. Keep that energy for this entire chapter.

HEADPHONES: SMALL BUT MIGHTY

If you plan to have guests on your podcast, it is critical for you to use headphones to limit the feedback. Sometimes when you play out their voice through your computer speakers, you may get feedback or other interference you don't want. As stated in the last section, your headphones do not have to be fancy. The headphones that came with your phone may work fine. If you have headphones that you used to listen to your Walkman back in the day, and they still work, that is also totally fine. The point is that you want to be sure that you hear the interview as it's coming through, without any noise interference.

As with microphones, I have a couple of different pairs of headphones. My travel set is a pair of Beats by Dre EP, a holiday present I received from my brother and sister-in-law. I take these with me on the road, and I also use them for music production and to DJ on occasion. I also have a pair of Sony 1000XMs, which were a total splurge. These help me the most with music production, as I can better hear low frequencies with them. But do you need them as a podcaster? Absolutely…NOT!

Occasionally, you may find yourself in a bind where you want to record a podcast episode and don't have any headphones. In such cases, have your finger on the mute button while recording. Just unmute, talk, and then mute yourself. This will also help keep your audio clean and feedback-free.

WEBCAMS: I'M READY FOR MY CLOSEUP

Now we're going to talk about webcams. This portion is completely optional because there are several platforms that you can use which do not require you to have a webcam. I  like webcams because I like to get the video as well as the audio, which gives me options. We will discuss repurposing content using video and other formats in Module Six.

Before we dive in, here's a mantra regarding the MVP: *Whatever works, whatever's available.* We're trying to get that MVP off the ground. No matter what I say, the most important thing is to get the info out. All of the rest of the polish is just bells and whistles. However, I will reiterate that clean audio is paramount because people will stop listening to you if it's hard on their ears or they can't hear you.

Other than that, consider using a platform with a webcam. Not only does it help you be versatile and repurpose your content, but even in audio-only situations, there may be some specific nonverbal cues that the webcam can help you pick up on—for example if there's a pause in conversation. Let's say that you're interviewing me. I'm talking, and I pause to get my train of thought. If we are on camera, you can interpret my body language instead of jumping in and cutting me off.

For the webcam, depending on your desired outcome, it's not mandatory to have a pretty-looking webcam. Anything will do. You can even use the built-in one on your computer. However, if you're trying to get fancy, check out the resolution! The higher the resolution, the better the video quality. Most webcams record at either 1080p or

720p, but there're some models that record at even higher resolutions.

Again, I'm a gear snob, and you may be too. I like my audio to sound a certain way and my video to look a certain way. Let me take a moment to shout out my friend, Claudio Zavala (@ClaudioZavalaJr on Twitter), who taught me about the Elgato CamLink 4K adapter. This device allows me to connect my DSLR camera to my computer and use it as a webcam. I only use it for special occasions, such as when I recorded the accompanying course to this book (check it out at edumatch.thinkific.com/courses and take 50% off with code COMMUNITYPODCASTING).

If you're going with a webcam, consider having a light ring. They range in size and price. Let's get a little geeky once again. I tend to do that from time to time. Two main light temperatures you need to know are 5600 degrees Kelvin (outdoor) and 3200 degrees Kelvin (indoor). Indoor light has more of an orange-ish hue, whereas outdoor light has more of a blue-ish type hue (Killam, 2017). Many light rings allow you to switch between 5600 and 3200 degrees to alternate between an outdoor and indoor feel. The one that I have at home is the

NEEWER 18" SMD LED Ring Light, but there are other light rings that you can get for a fraction of the price. Again, don't break the bank. Just go for what you know. Upgrade as you grow. (I'm a poet and didn't even know it.)

CHOOSING YOUR PLATFORM

We're just about at the finish line for this module, and we're going to spend a little time talking about platforms: where you choose to host your podcast.

Evaluating podcasting platforms can be tough, but don't worry! Here are some key things to consider when choosing the perfect platform for your audio masterpieces:

- Host with the most: You want a platform that will keep your files safe and sound, with plenty of storage space and easy access whenever you need it.
- Distribution: Make sure your platform has a solid distribution network that will help your podcast reach new listeners and be discovered by the masses. Some platforms have their own directories and apps, while others let you spread your wings to other big players like Apple Podcasts, Spotify, and Stitcher.
- All about the Benjis: If you're looking to make some moolah from your podcast, you want a

platform that offers advertising, sponsorships, and paid subscriptions.

- Easy peasy: The platform should be simple and straightforward, with a user-friendly interface for uploading, organizing, and publishing your episodes.

Keep in mind that some platforms are beginner-friendly and require minimal technical know-how, while others may require more advanced skills to maximize their potential. It all depends on your comfort level and goals for your podcast. There are even some with options for collaboration, integrations with other tools and services, and advanced customization options for your website, but they may not be necessary for every podcaster. Just assess your own needs and choose the platform that's right for you!

As for me, I started podcasting in 2008, and since then, I've gone through a few different platforms for hosting. The one I've done the longest, EduMatch Tweet & Talk, began in 2015. I used Podomatic, having used that as a DJ for many years. Then, I moved to Podbean for its unlimited storage and stayed there for a long time. (Some people also recommend SoundCloud for storage.)

There are several others about which I've heard really good things, such as Libsyn. However, whichever one you choose, make sure that it links with the major podcatchers, such as Apple Podcasts, Spotify, and Stitcher, to name a few. Anchor.fm, the one I'm using at the time of this writing, does this for you automatically. It's a free way to host your podcasts. I'll talk more about Anchor.fm in Module 4. (Skip ahead if you want the spoiler.)

I moved Tweet & Talk over to Anchor, as I had been using it for a podcast I did for my district and one that I did for my Master's students. I decided to switch because it also had unlimited storage, and even better—there was <u>no monthly fee.</u>

Once you choose your platform, I recommend putting out a teaser episode. Sometimes it takes a week or a few days for your podcast to get linked everywhere. A teaser episode, a little short bite, will ensure that your podcast will be linked and ready for your launch day. (More on that in a later module.)

HOMEWORK: WINDOW SHOPPING

Guess what time it is? It is homework time! Yes! All right!

For this module, you have two assignments. The first is to stop and take a mental inventory of what you already have or may need. I want you to think about your headphones. I want you to think about your microphone. I want you to think about your webcam (if you're going that route). Find them. Locate them. If there's something you don't have, now's a good time to order them.

The second thing is to look at the platforms I mentioned. Go in, research, and find out which one you think works best for you. What are the things that you like? What are the things you don't like? Share it in our community, and comment on other people's posts. We're going to figure this out together.

Take a look at all of the platforms that were mentioned in the *Choosing Your Platform* section. In our community, please respond to the following questions:

1. What are your initial thoughts?
2. What are the things that you like about various platforms?

3. What are the things you don't like?
4. Which one will you choose? No pressure...if you find that you don't like it later, you can always switch.

THREE

planning and preparation

Before we dive into Module 3, let's talk a little about teaser podcast episodes, the short and sweet previews that get your listeners pumped up for your full podcast series! Here's a checklist for what you need to think about as you prep for your teaser:

- Short and Sweet: Keep it short. Ruoff (2021) suggested adding why people should listen, and keeping it short—between 30 seconds to two minutes
- Get a Taste: Give your listeners a little taste of what they can expect from your full series. This could be a quick overview, a snippet of an interview, or some of your expert insights.
- Hook 'Em: Use your teaser episode to hook your listeners and get them hyped for your full series. Think cliffhangers, surprising twists, or dramatic scenes.
- Be On Brand: Make sure your teaser episode reflects your podcast's brand and messaging, including your logo, title, and any other visual elements.
- Share the Love: Share your teaser episode on social media and other platforms to reach more people. Use a catchy headline and link to your podcast website so people can check it out.

- Sound Quality: Make sure your audio quality is on point, sounding professional and building credibility with your listeners.
- CTA: End your teaser episode with a clear call-to-action, like asking people to subscribe or follow you on social media. Module 5 has more on Calls to Action.

Finally, Misener (2018) discussed the need for an evergreen teaser, which means your content is accessible and relevant to anyone at any time. For example, if somebody comes across your teaser a year from now, the information will still be as relevant as it was the day you posted it. Also, keep that in mind when you're thinking about episodes. This is not to say that time-sensitive information is something that you should always avoid. However, when you record evergreen shows, the content will be relevant to listeners for a long time. For this reason, be sure to omit references to dates and times.

Check out the teaser episodes of some of these popular shows for inspiration:

- "Serial" - This classic true crime podcast starts with a short and suspenseful teaser that sets the stage for the full series.
- "Stuff You Should Know" - This popular general knowledge podcast opens with a quick intro that gives listeners a taste of the hosts' humor and expertise.
- "How I Built This" - This entrepreneurship podcast starts with a short and inspiring clip of an entrepreneur telling their story, making you want to listen to more.

Remember, the key is to keep it short, sweet, and full of excitement for what's to come! By following this checklist, you'll create a killer teaser episode that gets your listeners pumped up for your full podcast series and brings in new subscribers. So, what are you waiting for? Get to planning!

WHAT TO EXPECT FROM THIS CHAPTER

If you've come this far, you have already completed a third of this book. This module will cover guests and topics for your show. We will begin with the importance of having a variety of guests, followed by the importance of crowdsourcing topics. We'll bring it home with some actionable steps, so stay tuned. Here it comes.

WHY CROWDSOURCE GUESTS?

Let's talk first about guests. Is your show going to focus on you as a solo host, or will you have guests? You don't have to be locked into one or the other, and you can switch up whenever you choose. One staple of EduMatch Tweet and Talk has been a crowdsourced panel of guests. But some episodes feature one person, and we go more in-depth. We even have a couple of solo episodes.

Shout out to my friend Dr. Will (@IAmDrWill on the socials), who has inspired me greatly in my podcasting journey. Sometimes he does a solo episode, and sometimes he does episodes with guests. Whatever you choose to do, it is your show.

If you decide to bring guests to your show, consider providing a variety of perspectives from many different demographic factors—location, role, gender, ethnicity, religion, or even various stakeholders such as students, educators, parents, and community members. It all depends on your show. However, speaking as a listener, I feel that podcasts are much richer when they present diverse perspectives.

Often, you hear a lot of the same people and a lot of the same ideas. But as a content creator, you are uniquely in a space where you choose what perspectives you want to elevate. Do you want to share someone's perspective or voice that has not traditionally been heard? You have that platform to do it. I encourage you to take this opportunity. There's nothing wrong with having someone who already has an established platform as a guest; however, it is also important to have variety so that your listeners can benefit from hearing a whole spectrum of voices and perspectives.

WHY CROWDSOURCE TOPICS?

The next thing is the importance of crowdsourcing topics. Like everything else in the book, this is optional. However, it can provide some relevance to your audience. You can regularly ask them things like, *what do you want to hear about? Do you want to suggest someone for the show? Do you want to come on the show?* I've seen some great podcasts do this. One that comes to mind is The BeerEDU Podcast by Kyle Anderson and Ben Dickson. They have a form on their website asking about topics and guests.

THE NITTY GRITTY OF CROWDSOURCING

When crowdsourcing potential guests and topics, you don't just stick to whom you know; you also find out who your listeners know or even who they are. This is cool. However, be intentional about the topics and people you choose. Ensure that guests and topics align with your podcast's mission and vision.

Sometimes you might get an outlier in your crowdsourcing, and you will determine whether or not the person or topic is a good fit. Not everything will be for everybody. That being said, something like a Google Form may be helpful for audience members to propose topics or sign up as potential guests for your show. Another helpful tool is Calendly, which links with Google Calendar. This comes in handy when it comes to scheduling and is freemium. At the time of this writing, the professional version, which I use, costs $12 monthly.

HOMEWORK: GOOGLE FORM

Google Form Template

bit.ly/podcastformtemplate

Homework time! Yay. This module's homework is optional. Click on the link or scan the QR code, and get the template to my Google Form. Then tweak it to create your own. When you are done, share the link in the community (bit.ly/communitypodcasting). You never know…you may find some great guests among your teammates!

FOUR

creation and workflow

We are now officially at the halfway mark. Before diving in, here are a couple more questions that may come to mind:

If you have a specific topic focus for your show, is it better to handpick guests or to crowdsource and ask them why they're interested?

That is a great question, and I think the answer is that it all depends on your goals and preferences. As I stated before, you could even do a little bit of both if you'd like. For example, with EduMatch Tweet and Talk, we often have a weekly discussion with crowdsourced topics, and it's open for sign-ups. In addition, we sometimes have special episodes. Sometimes these are people to whom I have reached out, and sometimes they reach out to me. So you can experiment with whatever works best for you, and remember, you can always be flexible when it comes to these matters. So it's all about what works for you and your show.

How far in advance do you schedule guests?

Again, this is entirely up to you. I prefer to do 30 to 60 days in advance to allow for flexibility, although it's not so far that you don't know what your schedule will be. However, sometimes this varies.

Without any further ado, let's dive in!

WHAT TO EXPECT

In this module, we will break down the recording and the editing process. We're not going to do a deep dive into either one, but I'll share with you some tips to get started. As always, you can always pop into the community with questions on what to do if you get stuck.

PLAN YOUR WORK AND WORK YOUR PLAN

The very first thing that you need to do is have a plan. As my dad used to tell me as a kid, "plan your work and work your plan." That's exactly what we're going to do. When you're getting ready to record, then you want to make sure that you have a plan for what exactly you're going to cover in your show.

Sometimes you might choose to have an outline to help you have a successful show. You can access a template by scanning the QR code on the next page.

bit.ly/episodetemplate

First, I'll put some information for the guest about how to connect to the episode. I'll also include the guest bio, so I can read it on air. (Some podcasters like to do this live, but some do it after the fact in an editing session, or sometimes they might even prerecord it. Find a workflow that works for you.)

Even if you're doing a solo episode, you may want to have a bulleted list of what you will talk about. It isn't necessarily a script to go word by word, even though some people use that format. If you choose to have guests, consider sharing your questions in advance.

A sample email where I share the document with a guest may say something like,

Hi _____!

I can't wait to connect with you on _____! Here are some questions that will guide our conversation. Please feel free to tweak as you see fit. Let's get together about 10 min before going live, to pre-chat. See you later!

Best,

Sarah

∾

With EduMatch Tweet and Talk, when doing crowdsourced panels, we often have a guest moderator, who comes up with questions. Before the show, they fill out a moderator Google Form where I get their bio and questions. Being that it is *Tweet* and Talk, I can also pre-schedule the questions to go out live on Twitter.

At this point, you may be wondering how to get started. The next sections describe a few tools that have worked well for me.

RECORDING

Anchor.fm

Hopefully, from our last homework assignment, you have found a platform that works for you where you want to host your show. Now, let's talk about recording.

Again, I use anchor.fm to host my podcast. But also, if you so choose, you can record directly within anchor.fm. They call themselves, "The easiest way to make a podcast." I can't say that definitively, but it has been easy for me.

One thing I love about Anchor is that it connects to major podcatchers with just the push of a button, whereas, with some other hosts, you'll have to go in and manually make the connections to all of these places. This can be time-consuming and complicated. However, Anchor connects directly to services such as Spotify, Apple Podcasts, Breaker, Google Podcasts, Overcast, Pocket Casts, RadioPublic, and Stitcher. You also have the option to put it in some other places as well.

You have the option to record straight from your browser or mobile device. Messages is another feature of anchor.fm that I like, where listeners can call in and leave a message using a link. You can then drag in their response and make it part of your show.

In addition, in the library, I can search all the audio that I've created or uploaded. Lastly, *transitions* features different sound effects that you can use in between. So it's very easy to record and put together an episode using anchor.fm. You can see a demo in action if you sign up for the Thinkific course (edumatch.thinkific.com/courses).

Streamyard

While Anchor is a great starting point, my absolute favorite service to record shows is Streamyard. It is a freemium (free and paid versions available) video tool that is housed on your web browser. I pay yearly for the Basic plan, which is a pretty penny (at the time of this writing, it's $240 per year). However, I feel as though the functionality warrants the price tag. With this service, you can livestream directly into several locations, such as Facebook, Twitter, YouTube, and more. You can also prerecord content and broadcast it at a later time.

The platform allows for six to ten on screen participants, depending on which plan you choose. I like to use it to stream into our Facebook group, YouTube page, and on Twitter. You can create custom announcements as well, directly in the platform.

What I love about Streamyard is that it is very easy to use, and seamlessly integrates the features of many of the tools we will discuss in the next section. Additionally, it has just the right amount of bells and whistles to leave you with a very professional-looking video. When you are done with an episode, you can also export the audio for easy podcasting. You can even boss up and integrate tools such as the Elgato Streamdeck, which allows you to do things like go live, navigate the platform, and display banners, all by pushing a button on a remote controller.

Soundtrap

Soundtrap is a popular online music and audio production software that will help you create podcasts on practically any kind of device, including Chromebooks. This freemium tool allows you to record and edit your podcast all in one place. When you are done, you can export your podcast from Soundtrap and add it to a podcast host.

So, you've recorded your show, but you want to give it that extra razzle-dazzle. What next? Fear not, friends…we will cover editing in the next section.

EDITING

Video

I've tried a few different things over the years, and my workflow varies based on the podcast that I'm doing. Before discovering Streamyard, I used a popular tool called Zoom. You may already be familiar with it, as many of us used it for remote learning during the pandemic.

Zoom is a freemium tool that allows for 100 participants. Paying for a Pro subscription (approximately $15 per month at the time of this writing) allows you up to 24 hours per meeting. There are other add-ons, such as Webinars, that allow you to go live on sites such as Facebook or YouTube, for an additional cost.

Whether you use Zoom, Streamyard, or another video service, you can take your recording and edit it. I use Final Cut Pro, but this may be overkill if you only use it to edit your podcast. If you're also using it for professional video editing, it might be right up your alley. However, if you're not, consider using iMovie or Camtasia, which are both a lot cheaper but provide similar functionality when it comes to podcasting. WeVideo is yet another web-based option.

Your goal when editing is to cut out anything that you don't want to appear in the final version of your podcast. I tend to be a minimalist in this area, but some folks prefer super-clean audio. Usually, I will cut out internet glitches, goofs, and the like. I used to be more meticulous and cut out pauses, but again, using Tim Ferriss's method, I trade off a tiny bit of quality for efficiency. When you are done with your editing, you can then export the video and the audio and use them on your various platforms. We will discuss getting the most bang for your buck in the final module, but for now, let's turn our attention to audio-only editing.

Audio

As I shared before, there are a few different podcasts that I have done in recent years—three specifically—one for EduMatch, one for my district, and one as a professor. The latter two followed a similar process, as they were either solo shows or the interviews were conducted face-to-face (pre-pandemic). I had no interest in using the video on these, and all I wanted was the audio. For these shows, I recorded directly into GarageBand or Logic (Mac). Many people swear by Audacity (Mac & PC), and some like to use Soundtrap as mentioned in the previous section. Whatever tool you use, the process is the same. Chop it up, take your final file, and upload the episode to your host.

So if you're not too worried about having a video per se, this might be a good option for you. You may want to record straight to Anchor, GarageBand, Audacity, or whatever tool you decide to use.

MORE PLATFORMS

There are a variety of podcasting tools on the market. Here are a few more that I have seen.

Zencastr is yet another freemium tool for podcasting. What I really like about it is that everybody records on their end. As a host, there's nothing more frustrating to me than when you lose audio because there is an internet glitch, and that happens All. The. Time. You then have to go back and edit it out, which can be a pain, especially in an otherwise perfect episode. Zencastr records the audio for each participant, so even if the internet cuts out, it is still recording. With Zencastr, you can get up to two guests for up to eight hours per month, and you can record in MP3. There's also a professional option with a 14-day free trial that you can check out. (Note: Streamyard has also added the functionality where it records for each individual guest.)

Squadcast.fm has a video component to it. In an earlier chapter, we discussed how visual cues can help group podcasts run smoother. I was first exposed to this tool as a guest and thought that it was cool to be able to see the people who were interviewing me, being able to feed off of their cues. Squadcast is a paid tool. Features include progressive upload so you'll never lose a recording, automatic backups, and WAV or MP3 files. (MP3 is pretty much all you would need, but WAV files are of higher quality.) Quite honestly, I would say that most people won't be able to tell the difference if you have a WAV versus an MP3, particularly in podcasting. However, it's always good to have options.

THINKING OFF-GRID

In the next two sections, we're going to talk about some special circumstances, such as having international guests. Some beta testers told me they were in opposite time zones from their guests. Depending on where in the world you are, sometimes it's night and day (pun intended). Some options to combat this are rooted in asynchronous conversations. Let's take a look at some asynchronous options.

Flip is one of the most popular educational tools out there, at the time of this writing. It is completely free for educators. It features single sign-on with Google, Microsoft, and other tools.

Once you are in, you can leave a prompt, and people can respond via video. You can then download these videos and edit them together. One suggested workflow is to have a grid for each episode and a different topic per question.

OUTSIDE THE VOX

My friend Jorge Rodriguez (@physednow on Twitter) created a podcast called The Voxcast. Jorge was initially in Texas, then relocated to the Middle East, so he and his co-hosts (shoutout to Justin Schleider, @SchleiderJustin on the socials) used Voxer to record their show.

Voxer is a freemium tool that functions like a walkie-talkie, but it saves the messages so you listen and respond when you can. It reminds me of those Nextel phones you might remember from the turn of the century. Wow, that sounds so old, right? Anyway, Voxer is available on the web, iOS, and Android. In the web version of the app, you can download the Voxes and edit them together, just as we discussed in the previous section with Flip.

HOMEWORK: THE TRAILER

This brings us to the end of module four, so now it's time for your homework. This module is really exciting because we're going to get our feet wet. I challenge you to make a very short teaser for your podcasts. This will run approximately two minutes or less and include information about who you are, what your show is about, what people can expect, and whatever else you would like to include. Then, I triple-dog-dare you to upload it as your episode zero. Finally, you will drop that link into the community so that we can all check it out and cheer you on. So are you ready? Get set, go.

Record a trailer for your podcast and upload it to your chosen podcast host. Share the link to our community (bit.ly/communitypodcasting).

FIVE

marketing and promotion

This module is all about sharing because sharing is caring. You have something to say; now it is time for the world to hear your voice. We will cover the importance of sharing and promoting, branding, show notes, and dropping your podcast in relevant spaces. Stay tuned.

QUICK TIPS

Reality check: Nobody will magically know about your podcast unless you share it. Shoutout to my friends Dr. Angela Dye and Scott Nunes, who both provided valuable feedback regarding the content and flow of the course that inspired this book. This brings me to a point about community. There are many education podcasters with so many different shows, and it is all a community. We all work together. The beautiful thing about this is that there are so many pieces to this pie. A new listener for one of us is a win for all of us because that person is now tuned into podcasts, and can go in and subscribe to as many different podcasts as they want. I wanted to give a nod to my peers. There are so many I could shout out; if I start, I will not stop. So, let's just continue to keep it rolling.

So one thing that Scott shared with me is about discovering your audience and adapting the content based on their needs and desires while maintaining your voice. How do you discover your audience? There are so many different ways that you could do this.

One great place to start is with your PLN (personal learning network). Also, some cross-collaboration can be very helpful. There have been many times when podcasters have appeared on each other's shows. For example, Dr. Dye, a great friend and thought partner, has been on an episode of EduMatch, and I've been on an episode of her podcast, *Empowerment Starts Here*. Another podcaster I have cross-collaborated with has been Dr. Will Deyamport, with his *Dr. Will Show*.

Leveraging our communities and leveraging the communities of our communities are great ways to discover your audience. Even though the numbers might not be there at first, the important thing is to be consistent. To be honest, I'm not the best example of this, so this is more of a *do as I say and not as I do*. However, for many years, we religiously did Tweet and Talks at 6 PM Eastern on Sunday nights, and the episode would drop as a podcast episode Tuesday at 5 AM.

This brings me to another point about work-life balance. Podcasting may be very exciting and new, but there needs to be a balance, or you will be at risk of burning out. It does not need to look the same weekly or monthly. There will be times when you can be hardcore and prepare many episodes, which can help tide you over in more hectic moments.

Dr. Sheldon Eakins (@sheldoneakins on the socials) shared with me that he generally has many episodes in the tank. Upon hearing this, I pre-edited ten episodes (one full season) worth of Tweet and Talk over a winter break. However, that pace was impossible to maintain during the course of the school year.

No one universal method is right. It is all about what is right for you and what is right for *you now*. You need to know about the season of your life where you are currently, which will change.

MAINTAINING YOUR VOICE, EVEN IN STICKY SITUATIONS

In our last module, I touched upon the importance of maintaining your voice. I want to give you a quick example of when keeping it real goes wrong. Every now and then, you may have a guest on your show where you all have drastically different viewpoints. Take it from me...think through how you will handle situations like that well in advance.

When it comes to podcasting, having difficult guests on the show can be a real struggle. But, handling them with grace is very important. If things do take a turn for the worse, stay calm and focused. No need to get into a heated discussion; instead stay in control of the interview and steer it back on track. If all else fails, don't be afraid to cut the interview short.

I have been in situations where people have said things that I disagreed with and found harmful. Your personality may be more assertive than mine, and you may ask them follow-up questions. But me? I froze like a deer in headlights. However, it didn't sit right with me to leave the questionable views unchecked and look like I were condoning them, so I removed them in post-production (editing). Some hosts may add a disclaimer that the views expressed by the guests are not necessarily the views of the host to protect your brand. This brings us to…

GRAPHIC DESIGN

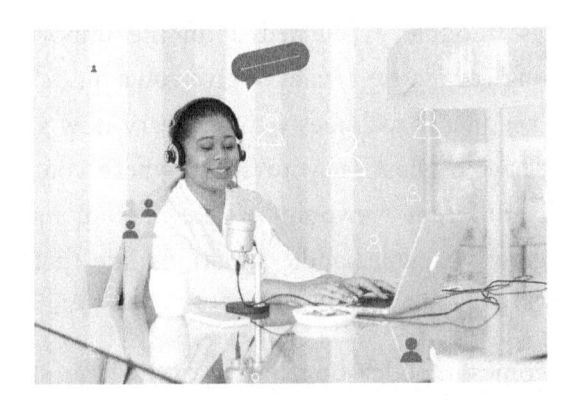

In this segment, we will be talking about some tools to make your life easier when it comes to sharing. The first is Adobe Spark. As an educator, you can get a free premium account. Spark allows you to create social graphics, web pages, and videos. The social graphics are already pre-sized for various platforms, with helpful templates for easy creation.

Canva is very similar, and features a drag-and-drop interface. It is also a freemium tool. But some of the stock images cost money to use. Canva also offers tutorials on its site to get you started.

Here's a Canva hack, courtesy of my friend Tammy Neil (@TGNeil on Twitter): some websites have royalty-free images you can access that do not require attribution and are free to use. Download your images from there and then bring them into Canva or Adobe Spark. A few of them that I like are Pexels, Pixabay, and Unsplash. There are many more, but those are great places to start.

BRANDING WITH FIVERR

Branding is all about creating a unique identity for your podcast that sets it apart and connects with your target audience. Here are a few things to consider when it comes to branding your podcast:

- Know Your Niche: What is your podcast all about? Who is it for? What makes it unique? Get clear on your niche, and make sure your branding reflects that.

- Establish Your Voice: Your podcast's voice should be consistent, authentic, and reflective of your target audience.
- Define Your Style: What kind of vibe do you want your podcast to have? What kind of imagery, colors, and fonts will you use to convey that?
- Create a Logo: A strong logo is key to establishing your brand identity and making it easy for people to recognize your podcast.

When it comes to information on branding, I highly recommend *Building a StoryBrand* by Donald Miller. This book is a game-changer and will help you understand how to create a clear and compelling brand message that connects with your audience.

My go-to for graphic design and overall branding is a website called fiverr.com, where you can buy services starting at $5. This online marketplace connects businesses and individuals with the best freelance services out there, including podcast branding. You can filter by categories such as logo types (e.g., 3D), output format, and many others. I would recommend that you get at least a PNG file for a logo, which will allow you to have a transparent background, as opposed to JPEG. Other options include PDF and Photoshop.

You also can filter for seller details, where you can see how highly people have rated the creator. I like to go with level two because they tend to be less pricey than the top-rated sellers, while still delivering high-quality products. I also like to choose people with many reviews.

You can also filter by country, but this does not make a huge difference for services like logo design. However, if I were ordering a gig for a press release, I might want to make sure that the creator lives in the United States instead of Canada or the United Kingdom because of the spelling differences. Some sellers, however, are well-versed in switching between various versions of English. Message them before buying the gig to ensure they can accommodate your specific project needs.

I have done things like podcast promos, introductions, bumpers, or drops through Fiverr.

- **Promos:** short audio clips that promote your podcast and encourage people to listen and subscribe.
- **Introductions:** the first thing people hear when they tune into your podcast, so it is important to make a good first impression! Consider having a theme song or other consistent way to kick off your show.
- **Bumpers:** short, sweet, and snappy audio clips that you can use to transition between segments in your podcast, or to give your listeners a little break before you jump into the next topic.

- **Drops**: pre-recorded audio clips that you can "drop" into your podcast to add some extra personality or to make a point. They can be anything from a sound effect to a jingle that you created specifically for your podcast.

You can even outsource your editing if that is not something that brings you joy. I am a huge fan of the site, and have been using them for years. I have had some great experiences (and some not-great ones), but I think it's worth the money to try it out.

SHOW NOTES

Now, we're going to talk a little about show notes. If you listen to podcasts, you probably see that some written content accompanies each show. Those are what are known as show notes. Show notes typically include information about the guest, the topic of the show, how to subscribe, and other relevant information. You can also add information and resources relevant to the episode.

Everyone's show notes are different. I have friends who provide extensive information on their guests and may even provide a transcript. While I think this is ideal, I am not the biggest fan of doing show notes. Once again, I use the Pareto principle. For me, less is more, so I provide very minimal information. But in your show notes, you can put whatever you would like. I'd highly suggest making a template that you can reuse for future episodes.

These notes are a great way to provide a preview to your audience. As a consumer, a lot of times, I'll browse show notes. If I have too many episodes in my queue, I'll look at the show notes and ask myself, "Do I really need to listen to this particular episode?" So the show notes are really good to keep in mind as you do your podcasts.

SOCIAL MEDIA SCHEDULERS AND MORE!

Once you have these social media posts and want to share them, there are also some tools that can help with that. Buffer is another freemium tool where you can preschedule your content to share on social media. Platforms include Twitter, Facebook, Instagram, LinkedIn, and more. You can easily share content on many sites at once. Just like an infomercial, you can set it and forget it. If you spring for the Pro version, you can "Rebuffer" your posts, saving you valuable time.

TweetDeck is similar; however, it only works on Twitter. This tool is free, which is my favorite word. I use this tool whenever we do a Tweet & Talk in order to preschedule tweets. Social Jukebox is another tool similar to Buffer and TweetDeck, and allows you to pre-set a scheduled interval for sharing.

A freemium tool that I found helpful for sharing promotional snippets was Wavve.co. The free version will allow you to create one minute of video monthly. The Alpha plan, which I was using, lets you do 10 minutes of video a month with no Wavve branding on your videos.

For more on social media tips, check out our course on social media for content creators (edumatch.thinkific.com/courses).

CALLS TO ACTION

And finally, the call to action. When you're listening to podcasts, the host might say, "If you like what you're listening to, then please subscribe, leave a rating, and tell your friends." That's what is known as a CTA (call to action), to which we referred in a previous module.

When you are sharing your podcast, it helps you build your audience base if you ask your subscribers to share it with their PLN or leave a rating or review. When people leave a rating, review, or share your podcast, this is known as social proof. Word of mouth is an effective marketing tool!

Here are a few possible calls to action:

- **Leave a Review:** Encouraging your listeners to leave a review on Apple Podcasts, Stitcher, or another platform can help boost your show's visibility and attract new listeners.
- **Join Your Community:** If you have a Facebook group, Discord server, or another community platform, encourage your listeners to join and connect with you and other fans of your podcast.
- **Visit Your Website:** Drive traffic to your website by encouraging your listeners to check out your show notes, learn more about you, or sign up for your email list.
- **Share Your Episode:** Ask your listeners to share your episode with their friends and followers on social media. You can even provide them with a pre-written tweet or post to make it easy!

For every educational podcast I listen to, I try to share it on Twitter with the hashtag #podcastEDU. Share new podcast episodes using that hashtag, and encourage your subscribers to do the same.

HOMEWORK: LOGO TIME!

For your homework, I would love for you to drop your show's logo into our community so that other people can see what you are working with. See you there!

SIX

the finish line

You made it! Congratulations for getting to module six. Here, we will discuss repurposing content. We will effectively attempt to get the most bang for our buck. So, without any further ado, we'll start with the first lesson.

CAPTIONS

As we discuss the ways to get the most bang for our buck, we also need to talk about accessibility. When I was rolling out the course, a beta tester told me that she appreciated the accessibility. Under each video, I included transcripts, which can make the content more available to those with hearing impairments. Captions actually help *everyone*. When I watch videos, sometimes I like to speed them up and just read the caption, especially if I am in a situation where I can't play the video out loud. They also help for the searchability and discoverability of your show. The next two sections will discuss tools I use for easy captions.

Rev

Rev.com does transcriptions, captions, and foreign subtitles. You may be wondering about the difference between transcriptions and captions. Transcripts write out the words you say, which you can see used in the course (edumatch.thinkific.com/courses). I copied and pasted all the words below the videos. Pro-tip: this may be useful for any doctoral students who need to transcribe interviews.

Captioning, though, is when you have the words blazed into the video. I tend to prefer transcription over captions because captions occasionally cover up video features such as lower thirds.

At the time of writing, the rate is $1.25 a minute for transcriptions and captions. With this tool, you have actual freelancers doing the transcription. There is an option to add a glossary of hard-to-pronounce or hard-to-spell words and phrases. Most transcripts will be completed within 12 hours.

If you use Rev or something high-quality such as this, your transcription could be used as a blog post. As a matter of fact, I used the transcripts from the course to help in writing this book and was able to get it done in three days.

All that being said, you always want to go back and make sure that the transcription is accurate. If you find something that is off, you can just go in and tweak it yourself.

Temi

You might have read the last section with the same initial reaction that I had. I thought, "Oh, this is really awesome. However, it's going to be kind of costly." If my show is 45 minutes long, I don't want to pay close to $60 weekly for a transcription. My friends, Temi is your solution. Temi is made by Rev and does the same thing, with the sole difference being that the transcription is done by artificial intelligence. Because it's a machine, it tends to make more errors. This is the tradeoff.

However, it may be worth it. Temi charges a fraction of Rev's price, $0.25 per minute instead of $1.25 per minute. So let's say I have a show that is an hour long. Temi will charge me $15 to transcribe it, as opposed to the $75 from Rev.

PAIRING WITH A TWITTER CHAT

Something else that you may want to consider in terms of getting your content repurposed is to include a Twitter chat, either occurring synchronously with the conversation (a la *Tweet & Talk*) or after the fact. For many years, Jake Miller (@JakeMillerTech on Twitter) did a podcast called *EduDuctTape*, where he would drop a weekly pre-recorded episode and then have a Twitter chat about it.

If you take the *Tweet & Talk* approach, you may want to consider having a guest moderator because otherwise, it becomes very hectic to go back and forth between the platforms. When you are a podcast host, then you want to be sure to be present and engaged. With *Tweet & Talk*, I come in, drop the intro at the beginning, and have everyone introduce themselves. And then bam, I hand it over to the moderator as I turn my attention to Twitter and Facebook, monitoring the conversation on those two platforms. Then, I bring in tweets or comments from Facebook into the chat, and finally, come on at the end and do an outro. During the actual show, I am listening, but I am only halfway paying attention. Therefore, especially if you are new to podcasting, consider doing an asynchronous chat or having a guest moderator on your show. This will free you up to monitor your backchannel, and have an even richer dialogue..

FINAL TIPS

We are family. I got my podcasters with me.

I wanted to leave you with a couple more tips before we officially close out and get to your final exam.

First, be an avid listener to podcasts. One way to level up is to listen to what our colleagues and peers are doing. I have gotten very good at speeding up podcasts so that I can consume them rapidly. This is an acquired skill that takes practice. However, don't be afraid to stop and smell the roses. There might be some that you slow down so that you can really absorb what they are saying as they are saying it. You may also want to take notes or bookmark things for later. But by all means, just keep listening. From there, you will discover various ideas that will help you improve.

I remember when I was at the gym one day when I heard an ad come through a non-education podcast. At the time, education podcasts typically didn't have many ads. So I started thinking about ways that I could amplify my PLN. I created a Google Form where listeners could send me a 30-second ad for free events for the educational community that I would drop as "commercial breaks." This was a win-win for all of us. So I would encourage you to subscribe and check out the podcasts of your fellow co-learners in this space. I look forward to subscribing to you as well.

The second tip is to continue to share with the community, so don't forget about #PodcastEDU. A lot of people click on that hashtag so they can discover new content. Also, retweet other people to whom you listen. Let's amplify one another and build one another up, while we build our audiences together. It's not a zero-sum game, so we are all here with the same goal in mind: to help our colleagues around the world get better at what we do. So let's continue to amplify one another. If you find some good content, then share it.

So that is a wrap—six modules down. You did it! Congratulations to you. Your final exam is to share your episode one. If you're already rocking and rolling, share your newest episode. Please listen and subscribe to one another, give each other feedback, and let's continue to build together. Keep in touch, everybody! Happy podcasting.

FINAL EXAM

Yay, you made it! Post Episode 1 (or the latest episode) to our community, and please listen to, subscribe, and share the work of your co-learners.

references

Anchor. (2019, November 8). *How to make a great podcast trailer*. Medium. Retrieved November 12, 2022, from https://medium.com/anchor/how-to-make-a-great-podcast-trailer-723cd159b89c

Clear, J. (2022, August 31). Continuous improvement: How it works and how to master it. James Clear. Retrieved November 12, 2022, from https://jamesclear.com/continuous-improvement

Ferriss, T. (2020, January 16). How to learn any language in 3 months. The Blog of Author Tim Ferriss. Retrieved November 12, 2022, from https://tim.blog/2009/01/20/learning-language/

Killam, R. (2017, August 17). *Color temperature explained*. 1000Bulbs.com. Retrieved November 12, 2022, from https://www.1000bulbs.com/land/color-temperature

Misener, D. (2018, November 20). *Every podcast needs a trailer - medium*. Medium. Retrieved November 13, 2022, from https://blog.pacific-content.com/every-podcast-needs-a-trailer-89f2f69c9847

Ruby, D. (2022, August 20). *39+ Podcast Statistics 2022 (Latest Trends & Numbers)*. Demandsage. Retrieved November 12, 2022, from https://www.demandsage.com/podcast-statistics/#:~:text=41%25%20of%20people%20in%20the,to%20a%20podcast%20every%20month.

Ruoff, M. (2021, December 21). *How to create the perfect podcast trailer*. The World's Audio. Retrieved November 12, 2022, from https://live365.com/blog/how-to-create-the-perfect-podcast-trailer/

acknowledgments

Writing this book has been a team effort in many ways. First, I would like to thank the beta testers of the course who provided feedback and helped the course take shape.

Next, I would like to thank my focus group. I chose you each for a specific reason, and appreciate your time, attention, and inspiration. Much love. In ABC order by last name: Dr. Will Deyamport, Dr. Angela Dye, Mandy Froehlich, Tara Linney, and Dr. Ilene Winokur.

Thank you to the members of EduMatch, particularly those who encouraged me to begin the *Tweet & Talk* Podcast. Tammy Neil coined the term "tweet & talk," and she, Amanda Lanicek, and Melissa Eddington initially proposed the idea. Thank you to our panelists, particularly those who have been on multiple episodes to share their perspective and expertise with the educational community.

To the Technology Training Team (T3) in my district, you all first introduced me to podcasting through the Sharing Technology with Educators Program way back in the day. I am forever grateful, and was honored to work on a podcast for the district with you. That was a full circle moment.

Thank you to the members of the EduMatch Publishing team who keep things running seamlessly: Mandy Froehlich, Desmond Hasty, Dr. Toutoule Ntoya, Martine Brown, Elissa Frasier, Dr. Casey Jakubowski, and Sara Oakland Bates. Also many thanks to Dr. Judy Arzt who is a phenomenal editor, among many other hats she wears. Finally, thanks to our authors. I have joined your ranks!

Thank you to the folks who created ChatGPT for helping me beef up my book (LOL)! Also thank you to the good people who share their work on Pexels, providing a great library of royalty-free images.

Last but not least, thank you to the educational podcasting community, including those who have picked up this book. It has been an honor to learn and grow with you, and I can't wait for even more great things to come.

about the author

Sarah Thomas, PhD is a Regional Technology Coordinator in a large district in Maryland. She is the founder of the EduMatch organization, which promotes connection and collaboration among educators around the world. Through EduMatch, Sarah has published several collaborative and individual books. EduMatch is also a recognized Google for Education professional development partner.

Sarah serves as President on the Board of Directors for EduMatch Foundation, Inc., a nonprofit that supports grassroots work of students and educators. In addition, she is a co-author of the ISTE publication series, *Closing the*

Gap, focusing on digital equity, as well as a Google Certified Innovator and trainer.

Sarah graduated from George Mason University with a doctoral degree in Education, and a concentration in International Education. She also holds a Master's degree from Howard University in the field of Curriculum and Instruction.

Sarah was designated an ASCD Emerging Leader in 2016, and was recognized in EdTech Magazine's *30 K-12 IT Influencers Worth a Follow in 2020*. She was named by the National School Board Association as one of the "20 to Watch" in 2015. She was part of the Technical Working Group that refreshed the International Society for Technology in Education (ISTE) Standards for Educators in 2016-2017, and in 2017, she received the ISTE "Making IT Happen" Award.

Find her on the socials at @sarahdateechur.

also by sarah thomas, phd

CLOSING THE GAP

Digital Equity Strategies for Teacher Prep Programs

NICOL R. HOWARD, SARAH THOMAS, REGINA SCHAFFER

CLOSING
THE GAP

Digital Equity Strategies for the K-12 Classroom

SARAH THOMAS, NICOL R. HOWARD, REGINA SCHAFFER

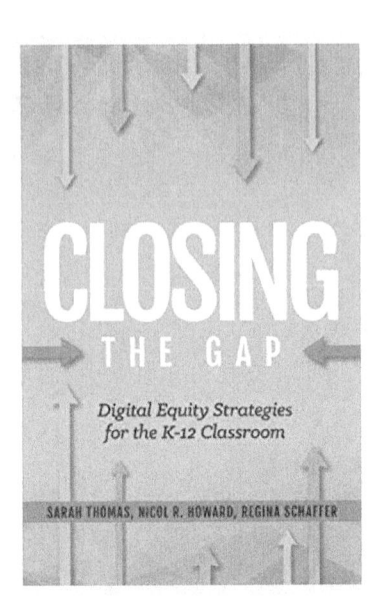

TO WHOM IT MAY CONCERN...

ESSAYS FOR EDUCATORS BY EDUCATORS

EDITED BY SARAH-JANE THOMAS, PHD
& NICOL R. HOWARD, PHD

#EduMatch SNAPSHOT in EDUCATION 2016

Contributing Authors (in order of appearance): Sarah Thomas | Tisa Simmons | Rachelle Dene Poth | Rachael J. Pierson | Bradford Hosts | Robert Ward | Tracy Brady | Roye Noad | Dene Gainey | Jodi Malerbi | Rolante Taylor | Stephanie Filardo | Christy Cate | Leslie R. Fagin | Neaal Kulawara PhD | Demetrius Ball | Sheela Lewis | Justin Schleider | Donald A. Madison | Josh Allen | Tammi Nell

---

The #EduMatch TEACHER'S RECIPE GUIDE

Survive and thrive in the kitchen and beyond!

Tammy Neil | Sarah Thomas | Demetrius Ball | Tracy Brady | Jennifer Casa-Todd | Christy Cate | Barbara Cotter | Tracy Klingbiel | Dan Kreiness | Stacy Lovdahl | Katie J. McNamara | Rachelle Dene Poth | Amy Storer | Kate Zaldivar

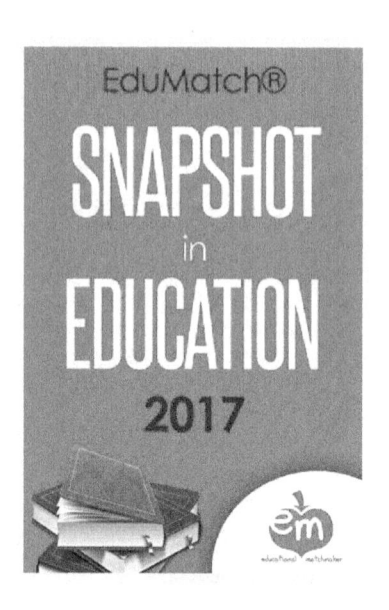

EduMatch®
SNAPSHOT in EDUCATION
2017

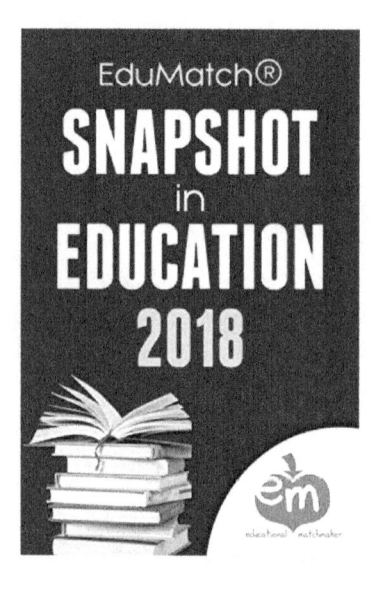

EduMatch®
SNAPSHOT in EDUCATION
2018

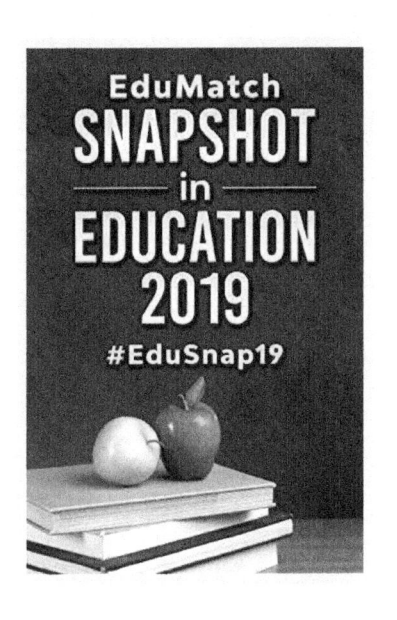

EduMatch SNAPSHOT in EDUCATION 2019
#EduSnap19

EduMatch® SNAPSHOT in EDUCATION 2020
REMOTE LEARNING EDITION

SNAPSHOT in EDUCATION 2022

EduMatch®

related edumatch titles

21 LESSONS OF TECH INTEGRATION COACHING BY MARTINE BROWN

Are you looking for strategies and techniques to take your practice to the next level by building digital capacity for teachers and instructional leaders? In *21 Lessons of Tech Integration Coaching*, Martine Brown provides a practical guide about how to use your skills to support and transform schools.

As a veteran, teacher, educator, and instructional coach, Martine shares her insights in a series of reflective lessons that expound on 21 key lessons that she has used to help hone her craft.

RELATED EDUMATCH TITLES

CLASSROOM TO CEO IN 30 DAYS BY ERICA TERRY

In *Classroom to CEO in 30 Days: An Educators Complete Guide to Starting a Profitable Online Side Hustle in One Hour a Day*, former teacher turned CEO Erica Terry equips you with a SIMPLE step-by-step system to start an online side hustle that requires little to no initial investment and is profitable from the very beginning. Together with lessons learned from her own experience transitioning from educator to edupreneur and those of featured guests from the popular Classroom to CEO Podcast, Erica lays out a plan for any educator to take the skills and knowledge that they use every day in their current role and turn it into a profitable online business.

Whether you're an educator looking to completely step away from the four walls of the building or you absolutely love what you do and are seeking a way to earn extra income, *Classroom to CEO in 30 Days* offers a proven framework for starting an online business, growing an engaged community and creating a life and legacy that you love by using your unique gifts and talents to empower others to achieve success.

RELATED EDUMATCH TITLES

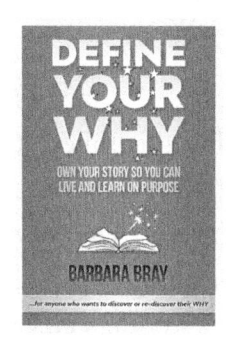

DEFINE YOUR WHY: OWN YOUR STORY SO YOU CAN LIVE AND LEARN ON PURPOSE BY BARBARA BRAY

Barbara Bray wrote *Define Your WHY* from the process she went through to figure out her WHY and through coaching others who did not feel valued, appreciated, or why they needed to live on purpose. Barbara tells her story with stories from 26 inspirational thought leaders along with quotes, resources, questions, and activities to help you on your journey to define your WHY so you own your story.

INSTRUCTION WITHOUT BOUNDARIES BY DR. MATT RHOADS, SHANNON MOORE, AND JANELLE CLEVENGER MCLAUGHLIN

Instruction Without Boundaries: Enhance Your Teaching Strategies with Technology Tools in Any Setting is about creating classrooms without physical and digital instructional boundaries so our students can have the opportunities to learn anywhere and at any time in our ever-changing world.

RELATED EDUMATCH TITLES

JOY WORKS BY DR. JOY

How do we sustain our joy as educators during challenging times? It is not easy. In fact, it takes intention, endurance, and bravery. Dr. Joy focuses on the importance of taking ownership of our joy and offers eight skillfully written lessons to support the journey. She provides an opportunity for readers to go through an authentic process, encourages insightful solutions, and values the voices of other educators. Get ready to put in the joy work!

JOURNEY TO BELONGING BY DR. ILENE WINOKUR

Journey to Belonging: Pathways to Well-Being is filled with self-reflection and the author's discovery about different stages of belonging (self, personal, and professional) that can influence how educators approach teaching and learning. Dr. Winokur's research-based explanations about belonging and well-being include why our highest goal is to leave a legacy and a better future for all.

RELATED EDUMATCH TITLES

MAKING PROFESSIONAL DEVELOPMENT MATTER BY DR. NICK SUTTON

Make Professional Development Matter! is a book that is aimed at helping every teacher, principal, superintendent or any other educator realize why professional development in their setting may not be having the impact that they desire. The author examines the relationship educators have with their personal lives and human nature to potentially improve professionally. This book provides a four-step process for building quality professional development plans, but does so through a combination of connections to established areas of research and also personal experiences through veteran educator Dr. Nick Sutton.

RELATED EDUMATCH TITLES

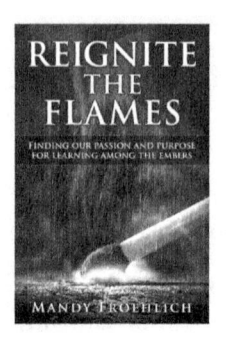

REIGNITE THE FLAMES: FINDING OUR PASSION AND PURPOSE FOR LEARNING AMONG THE EMBERS BY MANDY FROEHLICH

Reignite the Flames, the follow-up book to *The Fire Within*, expands on the concepts of:

• Educator engagement and disengagement

• The connection between disengagement and mental health issues like burnout, secondary traumatic stress, and demoralization

• The impact of stress and trauma on our brains and bodies

• And strategies for self-care and re-engagement

There is no denying the challenge of being an educator, but there are opportunities to re-engage and be happy. *Reignite the Flames* provides the vocabulary and the roadmap to help.

RELATED EDUMATCH TITLES

THE EDUPRENEUR: MAKING THE IMPACT AND THE INCOME BY DR. WILL (FILM)

The Edupreneur is a 2019 documentary film that takes you on a journey into the successes and challenges of some of the most recognized names in K-12 education consulting. The interviews feature eight edupreneurs discussing their lives and careers as educators and entrepreneurs.

SCRIPTED BY PAULA NEIDLINGER, BRUCE REICHTER, AND RANDALL TOMES

Scripted will serve as a resource book for all educators, providing a scope and sequence for digital media in the classroom written by three seasoned educators teaching in the digital trenches every day. The book provides classroom-proven strategies and resources, as well as trials, tribulations, and ideas to assist educators in building or adding to their existing digital media program.

RELATED EDUMATCH TITLES

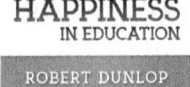

STRIVE FOR HAPPINESS IN EDUCATION BY ROBERT DUNLOP

This book will get you thinking about how happy you are in your career and give you practical strategies to make changes that will truly impact your happiness. Packed with research and inspiring stories, you will end each chapter inspired and excited to try new job-embedded ways to find more joy at work.

THE EXPERT EFFECT BY GRAYSON MCKINNEY AND ZACH RONDOT

The Expert Effect includes practical teaching strategies and QR code links to resources and templates that make it easy to integrate this system into your curriculum. Regardless of the grade level you teach, you'll find inspiration and ideas that will help you engage your students in an unforgettable way.

RELATED EDUMATCH TITLES

UNLOCK CREATIVITY BY DR. JACIE MASLYK

If you feel like you've lost your ability to be creative in the classroom or believe that student creativity needs a jumpstart, then this book is for you. It's for teachers who want to reimagine what teaching can look like in a creative classroom. It's for school and district leaders who recognize that students are more than test scores. It's for curriculum leaders and instructional coaches who want to rethink school curriculum by infusing creative opportunities for all learners. This book will provide tools for you as the teacher to increase your personal creativity as well as strategies to empower your students. This book is for anyone who wants to unlock creativity in powerful ways by unleashing our imaginations and create exciting possibilities for kids!

RELATED EDUMATCH TITLES

UNCONVENTIONAL BY RACHELLE DENE POTH

As educators, we have tremendous opportunities to create unconventional learning experiences for every one of our students. Sometimes we just need a push, some encouragement to let us know that we can do things differently, and think outside the box. *Unconventional* will empower educators to take risks, explore new ideas and emerging technologies, and bring amazing changes to classrooms. Dive in to transform student learning and thrive in edu!

#DIGITALPD FOR EDUCATORS BY DR. MATTHEW WOODS & DR. SAM FECICH

Growing and learning is a continuous process for everyone…including educators. Let us guide you through different digital professional development opportunities that can strengthen your practice and confidence in your classroom.

EduMatch

PUBLISHING

Made in the USA
Middletown, DE
30 April 2023